Slime, Poop, and Other WACKY ANIMAL DEFENSES

BY JANET RIEHECKY

CONTENT CONSULTANT:
JACKIE GAI, DVM
ZOO AND EXOTIC ANIMAL VETERINARIAN

READING CONSULTANT:
BARBARA J. FOX
READING SPECIALIST
PROFESSOR EMERITUS
NORTH CAROLINA STATE UNIVERSITY

CAPSTONE PRESS
a capstone imprint

Blazers is published by Capstone Press,
1710 Roe Crest Drive, North Mankato, Minnesota 56003.
www.capstonepub.com

Books published by Capstone Press are manufactured with paper
containing at least 10 percent post-consumer waste.

Library of Congress Cataloging-in-Publication Data
Riehecky, Janet, 1953-
    Slime, poop, and other wacky animal defenses / by Janet Riehecky.
    p. cm. — (Blazers. Animal weapons and defenses)
    Includes bibliographical references and index.
    Summary: "Describes how animals use slime, poop, and other wacky traits as defenses"—
Provided by publisher.
    ISBN 978-1-4296-6509-4 (library binding)
    ISBN 978-1-4296-8009-7 (paperback)
    1. Animal chemical defenses—Juvenile literature. 2. Glands, Odoriferous—Juvenile literature.
I. Title. II. Series.
QL759.R54 2012
591.47—dc23
                                                    2011034684

Editorial Credits
Mandy Robbins, editor; Kyle Grenz, designer; Svetlana Zhurkin, media researcher;
    Eric Manske, production specialist

Photo Credits
Alamy: Poelzer Wolfgang, 28–29; Corbis: Brandon D. Cole, 10–11, Visuals Unlimited/Jim Merli,
18–19; Dreamstime: Cathy Keifer, 4–5; Minden Pictures: Piotr Naskrecki, 12–13; Nature Picture
Library: J Downer Product/Simon Wagen, 8–9, Andy Rouse, 6–7; Photolibrary: Brandon Cole,
cover (bottom); Shutterstock: James Tibbott, 22–23, mikeledray, cover (top), Stacy Barnett,
16–17, Steve Heap, 20–21, Tiago Sá Brito, 24–25; Visuals Unlimited: Patrice Ceisel, 26–27;
Wikipedia: Zylornian, 14–15

Printed in the United States of America in
Stevens Point, Wisconsin.
102011   006404WZS12

TABLE of CONTENTS

CREATIVE DEFENSES

Animals try to avoid **predators**, but sometimes they get caught. Once caught, some animals do strange things to defend themselves.

predator—an animal that hunts other animals for food

GROSS OUT!

The Fieldfare thrush flies
above an attacker and poops
on it. The thrush's poop can
damage another bird's feathers
so badly that it dies.

★ FIERCE FACT ★

Many Fieldfare thrushes work
together pooping on predators.

A fulmar is a seabird. It **vomits** smelly stomach oil at attackers. The oil damages an attacker's feathers or hair. A fulmar can hit a target up to 8 feet (2.4 meters) away.

☆ FIERCE FACT ☆

Baby fulmars can spit oil even before they hatch.

vomit—to throw up food and liquid from the stomach through the mouth

A hagfish covers itself with sticky slime. **Glands** all over its body create the slime. It clogs an attacker's **gills**, damaging the animal's ability to breathe.

gland—a part of the body that produces fluids that the body uses or releases as waste

gill—an organ used for breathing by animals that live in water

An African foam grasshopper eats poisonous milkweed. The poison doesn't hurt the grasshopper. The grasshopper uses the milkweed to create poisonous foam. The foam oozes from the bug's leg joints when it is attacked.

Short-horned lizards collect blood in **valves** near their eyes. A lizard can shoot the blood as far as 3 feet (0.9 m) away. The blood stings the eyes of an enemy.

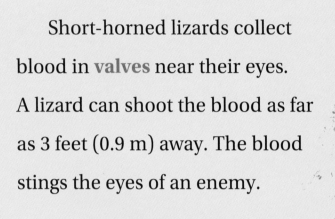

★ FIERCE FACT ★

Short-horned lizards also puff up their bodies to frighten enemies.

valve—a flap that opens and closes to control the flow of a liquid

PLAYING PRETEND

An opossum plays dead if it is attacked. It falls over and lets its mouth hang open. Its eyes freeze in a blank stare.

☆ FIERCE FACT ☆

The opossum poops when it plays dead. The bad smell makes enemies mistake it for a rotting body.

A hognose snake also plays dead if attacked. It flips over onto its back and goes limp. It can even cause a trickle of blood to run out of its mouth.

★ FIERCE FACT ★

If a hognose snake is flipped back over while playing dead, it immediately goes belly-up again.

If a predator comes near a killdeer's nest, the mother bird fakes a broken wing. It drags one wing on the ground to look like easy **prey**. The bird leads its enemy away from the nest to protect its young.

prey—an animal hunted by another animal for food

OTHER STRANGE DEFENSES

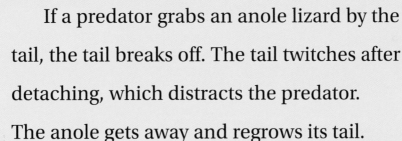

If a predator grabs an anole lizard by the tail, the tail breaks off. The tail twitches after detaching, which distracts the predator. The anole gets away and regrows its tail.

☆ FIERCE FACT ☆

Anoles have the ability to change color to blend in with their surroundings.

A starfish has many **limbs**. These limbs can break off to free it from a predator. The starfish then grows new limbs.

★ FIERCE FACT ★

Sometimes a starfish's broken-off limb becomes a new starfish!

limb—a part of the body used in moving or grasping

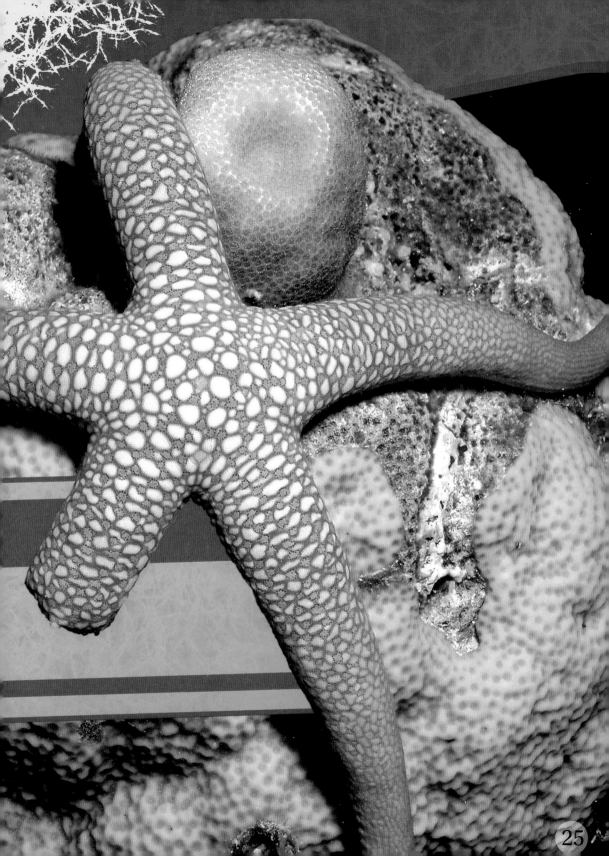

An electric eel can zap its attackers.
It has three organs that create an
electrical force field.

electrical force field—an area surrounding
something that has an electrical charge

★ FIERCE FACT ★

The charge of an electric eel is strong enough to knock down an animal as big as a horse.

★ FIERCE FACT ★

Some sea cucumbers can release poison through their skin.

Some sea cucumbers shoot
out long, sticky threads from their
bodies. The threads distract and
tangle up attackers.

GLOSSARY

electrical force field (ee-LEK-trih-kuhl FORSS FEELD)—an area surrounding something that has an electrical charge

gill (GIL)—the organ used for breathing by animals that live in water

gland (GLAND)—a part of the body that makes fluids that the body uses or releases as waste

limb (LIM)—a part of the body used in moving or grasping

predator (PRED-uh-tur)—an animal that hunts other animals for food

prey (PRAY)—an animal hunted by another animal as food

valve (VALV)—a movable part that controls the flow of liquid

vomit (VOM-it)—to throw up food and liquid from the stomach through the mouth

★ READ MORE ★

Brynie, Faith Hickman. *How Do Animals Stay Safe?* I Like Reading about Animals! Berkeley Heights, N.J.: Enslow Publishers, 2010.

Mitchell, Susan K. *Animal Chemical Combat: Poisons, Smells, and Slime.* Amazing Animal Defenses. Berkeley Heights, N.J.: Enslow Publishers, 2009.

Murray, Julie. *Disgusting Animals.* That's Wild!: A Look at Animals. Edina, Minn.: ABDO, 2010.

INTERNET SITES

FactHound offers a safe, fun way to find Internet sites related to this book. All of the sites on FactHound have been researched by our staff.

Here's all you do:

Visit *www.facthound.com*

Type in this code: 9781429665094

Super-cool stuff!

Check out projects, games and lots more at
www.capstonekids.com

INDEX